Basic Tips and Instructions for Woodworks for all Seasons

You'll love *these colorful all-year snowman characters for your home or as gifts for family and friends. Just follow out Never-Fail instructions to make a snowman and seasonal ornaments.*

Basic Materials:

Snowman body & base
Woodworks small parts
DecoArt® acrylic paints
Loew-Cornell paintbrushes
Clear acrylic sealer
Needle nose pliers

19 gauge wire
Brown floral tape
Small craft drill
Assorted trims
Lo-temp hot glue
Wood glue

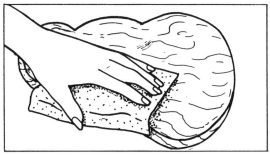

1. Sand Small Wood Parts with fine sandpaper or an emory board to remove rough edges. For easy assembly, use a craft drill for making holes in small wood parts.

2. Trace and Transfer Pattern. Trace pattern on tracing paper. Place transfer paper between tracing paper and wood piece, trace design with stylus or pencil.

3. Paint wood pieces following individual instructions. Make lettering with a liner brush and thinned paint or a permanent marking pen.

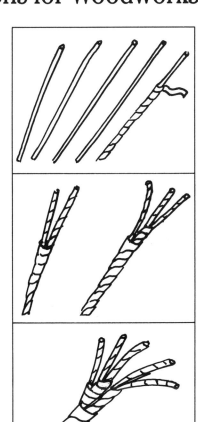

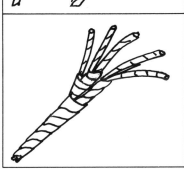

4. Assemble. Let paint dry thoroughly. Screw base on bottom of snowman piece. Glue wood pieces using wood glue. Glue embellishments with lo-temp hot glue.

5. Finish. Spray completed project with Clear acrylic sealer.

Branch Arm Assembly

1. For each arm, cut five 5" pieces of 19 gauge wire.
2. Wrap each wire with Brown floral tape.
3. Tape 2 wires together leaving 2" on one end.
4. Tape 1 wire to 2 wire set.
5. Tape remaining 2 wires together, tape to other wires.
6. Bend ends of wires as desired. Drill a ¼" hole in sides of snowman, glue wire arms in holes.

Paintbrush **Directory**

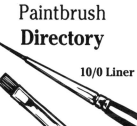

10/0 Liner

#2 Shader

#4 Shader

#12 Shader

3/4" Shader

Snowman

MATERIALS:

Pink powdered blush
8" of jute
Ribbed top of a Red sock
Scotties Antiquing Patina
Disposable plastic tray
Natural raffia

1" x 30" strip of Red/Tan fabric
Snow-Tex
Burnt Umber oil paint
Palette knife
Lint free cloth
Black Fine-tip permanent pen

WOOD PARTS:

Large snowman and base
½" button
1½" primitive heart
2" country star
2 acorns
Bird
Gingerbread girl

Three 1" star buttons
2¾" primitive heart
2 mittens
1¼" country star
4 carrots
Gingerbread boy

DECOART PAINT:

Buttermilk	Snow White	Ebony Black
Leaf Green	Antique Gold	French Grey Blue
Glorious Gold	Cranberry Wine	Rookwood Red
Pumpkin	Hauser Dark Green	Santa Red
Burnt Sienna	Uniform Blue	Gooseberry Pink
Yellow Ochre	Cadmium Yellow	Lemon Yellow

INSTRUCTIONS:

Trace pattern. Sharpen point of ¼" dowel for nose. Drill ¼" hole in face and one on each side of Snowman for arms. Glue nose in face hole, let dry.

PAINT:

Snowman

Body, base - Buttermilk, spatter Burnt Umber.
 Antique - Squeeze a dime size amount of Burnt Umber oil paint on tray, mix with one tablespoon of patina using palette knife. Paint on body with sponge brush, rub off with rag. Rub edges with a small amount of Burnt Umber oil paint.
Eyes, mouth - Ebony Black. Dot eyes Snow White.
Cheeks - rub with blush.
Nose - Pumpkin.
Star buttons - one each Rookwood Red, Cadmium Yellow and Hauser Dark Green.
Bird - French Grey Blue, shade wing Uniform Blue.
 Beak - Cadmium Yellow.
 Eye - dot Cadmium Yellow, add tiny Ebony Black dot.
Large heart - Hauser Dark Green, using thinned Yellow Ochre, paint checks.
Small heart - Rookwood Red.
 Stitches - Buttermilk.
Small button - Yellow Ochre.

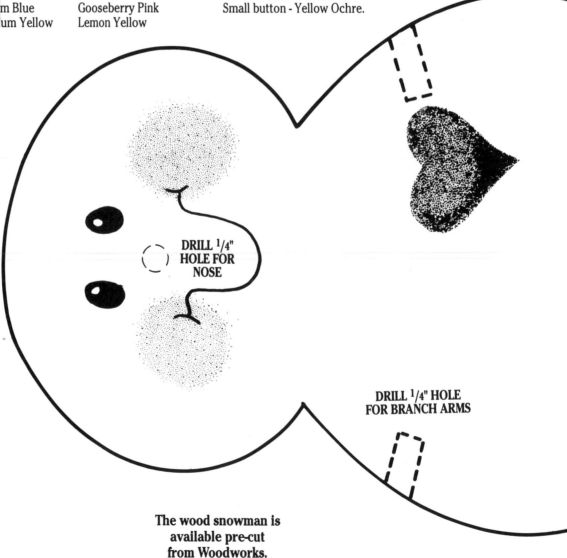

DRILL ¼" HOLE FOR NOSE

DRILL ¼" HOLE FOR BRANCH ARMS

The wood snowman is available pre-cut from Woodworks.

Country stars - Yellow Ochre, shade antique Gold, drybrush
Snow White.
Stitches - Black pen
Eyes, Eyebrows - Ebony Black..
  Brush with Clear sealer, sprinkle with Glamour Dust.
Mittens - French Grey Blue, shade Uniform Blue.
  Plaid - Snow White, wash French Grey Blue stripe. Add stripes
    with thinned Uniform Blue, outline Rookwood Red.
Gingerbread boy and girl - Burnt Umber, drybrush Snow White.
  Eyes - dot Ebony Black
  Buttons, dot Rookwood Red.
  Icing - Gooseberry Pink.
Acorns
  Bottom - Burnt Umber, shade Ebony Black.
  Top - Antique Gold, sponge Burnt Umber.
Corn (carrots)
  Husk - Leaf Green, shade Ebony Black.
  Kernels - Lemon Yellow, shade Cadmium Yellow. Line Ebony
    Black.

CUT 1
FROM 3/4"
PINE

ASSEMBLE:
Attach base to Snowman. Spread Snow-Tex around base of snowman and on top of base piece, let dry. Make arms, glue in side
holes. Tie jute around sock piece, glue on head for hat. Tie raffia
bow. Glue small heart, bow and button on large heart. Insert screw
eyes in small wood pieces referring to photo, thread raffia through
eyes, tie ends in a bow and hang on arms.

CUT FROM 3/4"
PINE

Ornaments for Snowman

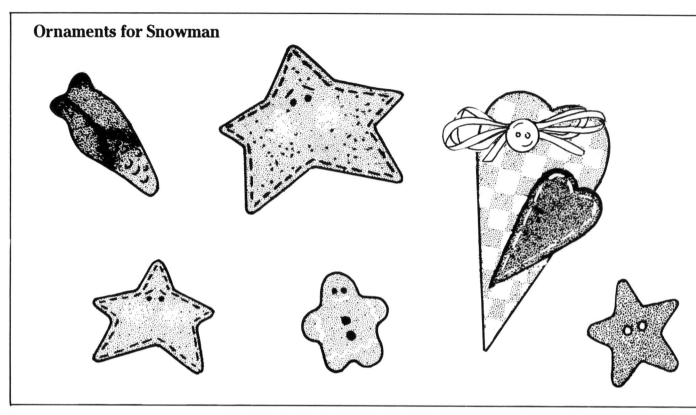

Glossary of Paint Terms

HIGHLIGHT-To lighten an area with the next lighter color value.

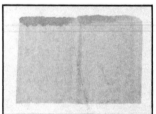

WASH-The application of transparent color made with a mixture of equal parts water and paint.

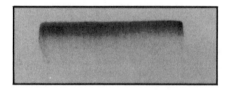

FLOAT or SIDE LOAD-Dip a flat brush in water. Blot on paper towel leaving some water in brush. Dip one side in paint. Stroke up and down on palette until color graduates to clear water on one side. Float color.

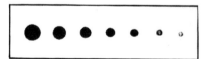

DOT-To apply paint with a stylus or the handle of a brush.

SHADE-A technique used to darken painted areas. A darker hue is applied over a lighter hue.

SPONGE-Wet sponge and remove excess water. Dip in paint, blot on paper towel then apply to surface.

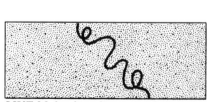

DRYBRUSH-A technique to shade or highlight an area. Color is applied with a brush which is almost free of paint.

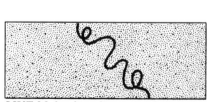

LINE-Make fine lines to define an area using a liner brush. Dilute paint with water to the consistency of ink.

STIPPLE-Using an old brush or a sponge, pounce color on an area repeatedly.

Color Conversion Chart

DECOART	DELTA	ACCENT	PLAID (Folk Art)
Antique Gold	Antique Gold + Raw Sienna	Yellow Ochre	Teddy Bear Tan
Burnt Orange	Georgia Clay	Sedona Clay	Persimmon
Burnt Sienna	Candy Bar	Burnt Sienna	Raspberry Wine + Burnt Umber
Burnt Umber	Burnt Umber	Burnt Umber + Burnt Sienna	Burnt Umber
Buttermilk	Antique White	Off White	Tapioca
Cadmium Orange	Orange	True Orange + Pure Red	Glazed Carrots + Calico Red
Cadmium Yellow	Yellow	Pure Yellow	School Bus Yellow
Cranberry Wine	Mendocino + Burnt Umber	Bordeaux	Raspberry Wine
Deep Midnight Blue	Nightfall	Soldier Blue	Heartland Blue
Desert Sand	Sandstone	White + Wicker + Apricot Stone	Clay Bisque
Ebony Black	Black	Ebony	Licorice
French Grey Blue	Midnight + White	Stoneware Blue	Settler's Blue
Glorious Gold	Metallic Gold	Brass	Pure Gold
Gooseberry Pink	Gypsy Rose	Pueblo Red + Apricot Stone	Salmon
Hauser Dark Green	Deep River	Teal Deep	Wintergreen
Leaf Green	Green Isle	Holiday Green	Shamrock
Lemon Yellow	Luscious Lemon	Yellow Light	Yellow Light
Light Cinnamon	Autumn Brown	Burnt Sienna	Nutmeg
Moon Yellow	Old Parchment	Devon Cream	Buttercup
Plum	Grape	Plum	Plum Pudding
Pumpkin	Pumpkin	True Orange + Lt Cactus Flower	Glazed Carrots
Raw Umber	Dark Chocolate	Burnt Umber	Raw Umber
Rookwood Red	Candy Bar	Barn Red	Apple Spice
Sable Brown	Territorial Beige	Raw Sienna + White	Honey + Chocolate Fudge
Santa Red	Tompte Red	Crimson	Napthol Crimson
Slate Grey	Bridgeport	April Showers + Black	Whipped Berry
Snow White	White	Titanium White	Titanium White
Tangerine	Bittersweet	True Orange + Dijon Gold	Tangerine
True Ochre	Antique Gold	Yellow Ochre	Yellow Ochre
Uniform Blue	Nightfall	Soldier Blue	Denim Blue
Yellow Light	Bright Yellow	Yellow Light	Yellow Light
Yellow Ochre	Cloudberry + White	Wild Honey + Tumbleweed	Camel

Note: Color matches may not be exact, a close color is indicated

Crystal Twinkles
Glamour Dust
Snow-Tex
Weathered Wood

Snow Santa

CENTER PHOTO

MATERIALS:

Pink powdered blush
Off White curly hair
Dried greenery
Black fine-tip permanent pen

Glamour Dust
Santa suit and hat
Green raffia

WOOD PARTS:

Large snowman and base
Two 1½" blocks
Two 1¾" circles
1½" of ¼" dowel

3 stockings
1¼" block
Two ¾" hearts
6 screw eyes

DECOART PAINT:

Buttermilk
Burnt Umber
Uniform Blue
French Grey Blue
Santa Red

Snow White
Rookwood Red
Cadmium Yellow
Glorious Gold
Slate Grey

Ebony Black
Antique Gold
Hauser Dark Green
Burnt Sienna
Leaf Green

INSTRUCTIONS:

Trace pattern. Sharpen point of ¼" dowel for nose. Drill ¼" hole in face and one on each side of Snowman for arms. Glue nose in face hole, let dry.

PAINT:

Santa

Body - Buttermilk, shade French Grey Blue.

Eyes - Ebony Black, float Buttermilk in lower part. Add star highlight on right side with thinned Buttermilk.

Cheeks - rub with blush.

Nose - Pumpkin, shade base Rookwood Red.

Mouth - dot Ebony Black.

Heart - Cranberry Wine, shade Cranberry Wine + Ebony Black. When dry, brush on Clear sealer, sprinkle with Glamour Dust.

Gold ornament - Glorious Gold, shade Burnt Sienna. Line Santa Red, stroke and dot Hauser Dark Green. Drybrush Snow White.

Red ornament - Santa Red, shade Santa Red + Ebony Black. Line Hauser Dark Green, stroke Glorious Gold. Drybrush Snow White.

Tree stocking - Buttermilk, shade Antique Gold.

Heel, toe - line Santa Red, dot Hauser Dark Green. Shade Cranberry Wine.

Tree - Hauser Dark Green, dot Rookwood Red.

Fur - stipple Slate Grey and Snow White.

Stitches, letters - Black pen.

Striped stocking - Hauser Dark Green, line Buttermilk.

Heel, toe - Buttermilk, dot Rookwood Red.

Fur - stipple Slate Grey and Snow White.

Stitches, letters - Black pen.

Plaid stocking - Rookwood Red, shade Rookwood Red + Ebony Black.

Heel, toe - line Hauser Dark Green and Rookwood Red.

Fur - stipple Slate Grey and Snow White.

Stitches, letters - Black pen.

Gold present - Antique Gold, shade Burnt Sienna.

Ribbon - Santa Red, shade Ebony Black.

Green present - Leaf Green, shade Ebony Black.

Bow (hearts), ribbon - Glorious Gold, shade Burnt Sienna.

Red present - Santa Red, shade Ebony Black.

Ribbon - Hauser Dark Green, dot and line Glorious Gold.

Base - Santa Red, sponge Buttermilk.

Checks - Buttermilk and Santa Red, shade Santa Red + Ebony Black.

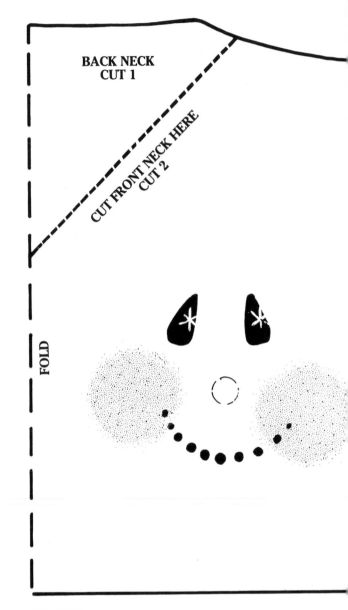

SANTA'S COAT
CUT FROM RED FOLK-ART FE[

BACK NECK
CUT 1

CUT FRONT NECK HERE
CUT 2

FOLD

ASSEMBLE:

Attach base to Santa. Make arms, glue in side holes. Glue coat an[hat on Santa. Glue curly hair on face for beard. Glue presents an[greenery on base referring to photo. Screw eyes in ornaments an[stockings, thread raffia through eyes, tie ends in a bow and han[on arms. Spray with Clear sealer.

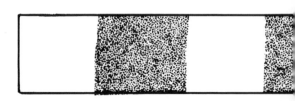

BASE

Scarecrow

CENTER PHOTO

MATERIALS:

Raffia	Pine cones
Dried fruit	Cinnamon sticks
6" straw hat	Small hay bale
Glamour Dust	5 screw eyes
Pink powdered blush	

Small bunch of dried flowers in autumn colors

WOOD PARTS:

Large snowman and base	Two 2¼" apples
Medium apple	3 maple leaves
3 acorns	1 sign
2 carrots	Bird
4" of ⅛" dowel	1½" of ¼" dowel

DECOART PAINT:

Buttermilk	Burnt Orange	Cranberry Wine
Leaf Green	Antique Gold	French Grey Blue
Snow White	Ebony Black	Pumpkin
Rookwood Red	Lemon Yellow	Cadmium Yellow
Tangerine	Santa Red	Burnt Umber
Weathered Wood		

INSTRUCTIONS:

Trace pattern. Sharpen point of ¼" dowel for nose. Drill ¼" hole in face and one on each side of scarecrow for arms. Drill ⅛" holes in base and bottom of sign. Glue nose in face hole, let dry.

PAINT:

Scarecrow
  Body - Buttermilk, shade French Grey Blue.
  Eyes - Ebony Black, float Buttermilk in lower part.
  Cheeks - rub on blush.
  Nose - Pumpkin, shade base Rookwood Red.
  Mouth - dot Ebony Black.
  Heart - Cranberry Wine.
When dry, brush on Clear sealer and sprinkle with Glamour Dust.
Pumpkins - Pumpkin, shade Burnt Orange, highlight Cadmium
    Yellow.
  Vines - Leaf Green.
  Stems - Burnt Umber.
Crow - Ebony Black, highlight wings Snow White.
  Stitches - Snow White.
  Beak - Antique Gold.
  Eyes - dot Antique Gold, add tiny Ebony Black dot.
Sign - Burnt Umber, let dry. Paint with Weathered Wood, let dry.
Paint with Buttermild. Let dry.
  Letters - thinned Pumpkin, outline left side Ebony Black.
Red leaf - Rookwood Red, highlight ends Santa Red.
Orange leaf - Antique Gold, highlight Rookwood Red.
Yellow Leaf - Lemon Yellow, shade Tangerine.
Acorns
  Bottom - Burnt Umber, shade Ebony Black.
  Top - Antique Gold, sponge Burnt Umber.
Corn (carrots)
  Husk - Leaf Green, shade Ebony Black.
  Kernels - Lemon Yellow, shade Cadmium Yellow. Line Ebony
    Black.
  Base - Buttermilk, sponge with Lemon Yellow and Pumpkin.

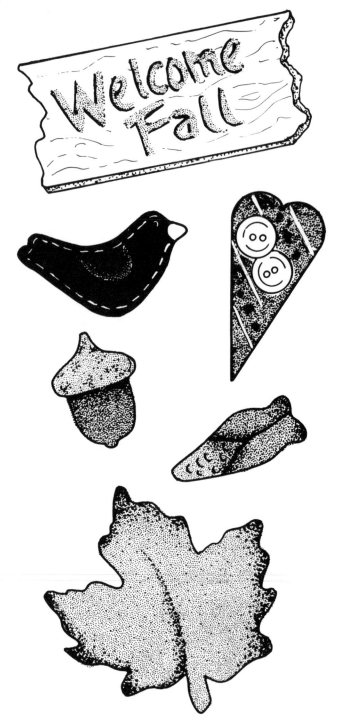

ASSEMBLE:

Attach base to scarecrow. Make arms, glue in side holes. Glue ⅛" dowel in sign and base. Glue leaves, pumpkins, acorn and bird referring to photo. Glue flowers, hay bale and pine cones on base. Cut several lengths of raffia for hair, glue on head. Place hat on head, glue. Wire dried fruit and cinnamon sticks together, twist ends of wire and bend wire over arms. Screw eyes in remaining small wood pieces, thread raffia through eyes, tie a bow and hang on arms. Spray with sealer.

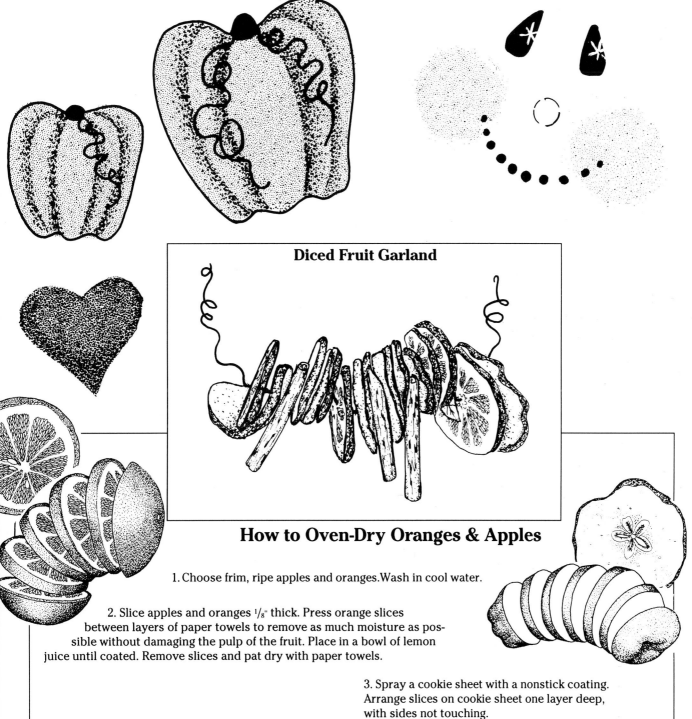

Diced Fruit Garland

How to Oven-Dry Oranges & Apples

1. Choose frim, ripe apples and oranges. Wash in cool water.

2. Slice apples and oranges ⅛" thick. Press orange slices between layers of paper towels to remove as much moisture as possible without damaging the pulp of the fruit. Place in a bowl of lemon juice until coated. Remove slices and pat dry with paper towels.

3. Spray a cookie sheet with a nonstick coating. Arrange slices on cookie sheet one layer deep, with sides not touching.

4. Place sheet in a warm 175° oven 3-5 hours for apples and 4-6 hours for oranges. Turn and check slices every 30 minutes. If fruit appears to be turning brown or become brittle, the oven temperature is too hot. Turn oven off for 15-30 minutes allowing fruit to dry more slowly. Turn oven on again and continue process.

5. Remove fruit and allow to cool completely. Apple slices should be pliable and leathery, but not moist. Lightly pinch orange pulp between fingers. If pulp contains moisture or slices are damp to the touch, continue oven-drying or allow fruit to finish air drying in a warm, airy place. Drying time varies according to humidity.

6. Spray fruit with a light coating of Activa Clear Glaze shellac or hairspray to seal from humidity.

An Angel to watch over thee

While Visions of Sugar Plums danced in their heads...

Snow Angel

CENTER PHOTO

MATERIALS:

6" grapevine wreath	Jute
White floral tape	12" x 24" of muslin
House and Tree stencils	Stencil brush
Pink powdered blush	Spanish moss
Black fabric pen	Glamour Dust
Large eye needle	2 screw eyes
24" of 19 gauge wire	

WOOD PARTS:

Large snowman and base	Wing
Three 2" primitive hearts	Three 2" primitive hearts
Two 2¾" primitive hearts	Two 1⅛" primitive stars
3 small primitive stars	Two ¾" buttons
Four ½" buttons	3 small primitive heart buttons
1½" of ¼" dowel	

DECOART PAINT:

Buttermilk	Snow White	Ebony Black
French Grey Blue	Rookwood Red	Pumpkin
Burnt Sienna	True Ochre	Hauser Dark Green

INSTRUCTIONS:

Trace pattern. Sharpen point of ¼" dowel for nose. Drill ¼" hole in face and one on each side of angel for arms. Drill ⅛" holes in one large, 2 medium and 2 small primitive hearts and large primitive stars. Glue nose in face hole, let dry.

PAINT:

Angel, wings - Buttermilk, shade French Grey Blue.

Eyes - Ebony Black, float Buttermilk in lower part. Add star highlight on right side with thinned Buttermilk.

Cheeks - rub on blush.

Nose - Pumpkin, shade base Rookwood Red.

Mouth - dot Ebony Black.

When dry, brush with Clear sealer and sprinkle with Glamour Dust.

Large buttons, heart buttons, large drilled heart, drilled small hearts, small heart, medium heart - Rookwood Red.

Stitches on small heart - True Ochre.

Medium heart - stripe Buttermilk, add Hauser Dark Green dots.

Medium drilled hearts, large heart - Hauser Dark Green.

Checks on large heart - True Ochre.

Large stars, small stars - True Ochre, shade Burnt Sienna.

2 small buttons - Hauser Dark Green.

2 small buttons - True Ochre.

Spray with Clear sealer.

DRESS:

Stitch seams on 12" side of muslin using a ⅝" seam allowance leaving 3" at top open. Place seam at center back, cut arm opening 3" from top. Turn under seam allowance at top, bottom and arm holes of dress, stitch. Stencil trees Hauser Dark Green, one house Rookwood Red with Yellow Ochre roof and two houses Yellow Ochre with Rookwood Red roofs. Write saying with fabric pen. Run 18" of jute through neck seam, place dress on doll and pull jute to gather, tie off

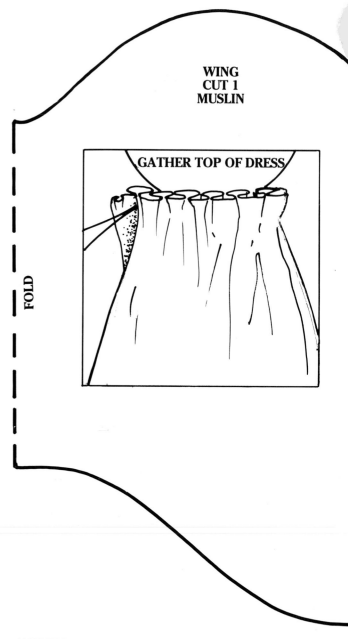

WING
CUT 1
MUSLIN

GATHER TOP OF DRESS

FOLD

ASSEMBLE:

Attach base to angel. Make arms, glue in side holes. Glue one small button and large buttons on wings. Glue wings on back of dress. Glue moss hair on head. Glue wreath on hair and small stars on wreath. Tie jute bow, glue on dress. Glue heart buttons on bow and Yellow Ochre houses. Tie raffia bow. Glue small button on raffia bow and bow and small heart with stitches on checked heart. Glue 2 buttons on striped heart. Screw eyes in checked and striped hearts, hang on arms. Thread drilled hearts and stars evenly spaced on wire, twist to secure. Curl wire between each piece around dowel. Bend wire ends over arms.

An Angel to watch over thee.

HEART & STAR GARLAND

Gingerbread Man
CENTER PHOTO

MATERIALS:

Pink powdered blush   Glamour Dust
Crystal Twinkles   Raffia

WOOD PARTS:

Large snowman and base
Four 1" round disks   7 small teardrops
Five 2¾" primitive hearts   Two 1¼" x 3" rectangles
Four 1¾" x ⅛" hearts   3 drilled gingerbread boys
2 drilled gingerbread girls   36" of ⅛" dowel
1½" of ¼" dowel   4 screw eyes

DECOART PAINT:

Buttermilk	Snow White	Ebony Black
Gooseberry Pink	Cadmium Orange	Raw Umber
Pumpkin	Leaf Green	Santa Red
Yellow Ochre	Slate Grey	Antique Gold
Lemon Yellow	Plum	
Cranberry Wine	Rookwood Red	Santa Red

INSTRUCTIONS:

Trace pattern. Sharpen point of ¼" dowel for nose. Drill ¼" hole in face and one on each side of gingerbread man for arms. Glue rectangles together for sign. Drill ⅛" holes in primitive hearts, sign and base referring to pattern. Cut ⅛" dowel into 2¾", two 4", 5½" and 6" lollipop sticks and a 2" sign pole. Glue nose in face hole, let dry.

PAINT:

Gingerbread Man
  Body - Yellow Ochre, shade Antique Gold. Stipple Snow White.
  Eyes - Ebony Black, float Buttermilk in lower part. Add star highlight on right side with thinned Buttermilk.
  Cheeks - rub with blush.
  Nose - Pumpkin, shade base Rookwood Red.
  Mouth - dot Ebony Black.
  Heart - Cranberry Wine, shade Cranberry Wine + Ebony Black.
Lollipops (primitive hearts)
  2 Green - Leaf Green, shade leaf Green + Ebony Black.
  1 Plum - Plum, shade with Plum + Ebony Black.
  1 Red - Santa Red, shade Santa Red + Ebony Black.
  1 Orange - Cadmium Orange, shade Cadmium Orange + Ebony Black.
  Sticks - Snow White.
Gumdrops (teardrops)
  2 Red - Santa Red.
  2 Yellow - Lemon Yellow.
  3 Orange - Cadmium Orange
  Brush with Clear sealer, sprinkle with Glamour Dust.
Peppermints (disks) - Snow White, stripe Santa Red. Shade Slate Grey, drybrush Snow White.
Sign - Buttermilk
  Lines - thinned Santa Red, shade Raw Umber.
  Letters - Black pen.
  Pole - Santa Red, shade ends Ebony Black.
Cookies & Gingerbread Kids (1¾" hearts, drilled boys and girls)
  Cookies, kids - Yellow Ochre, shade Antique Gold. Line with thinned Gooseberry Pink.

Eyes & Mouth - dot Ebony Black
  Heart - Cranberry Wine, highlight Snow White. When dry, brush Clear sealer and sprinkle with Crystal Twinkles.
Base - Buttermilk, shade Raw Umber.
  Checks - Santa Red, shade Raw Umber.

ASSEMBLE:

Attach base to gingerbread man. Make arms, glue in side holes. Glue sticks in lollipops and pole in sign. Glue pole and sticks in base. Glue gumdrops and peppermints in place referring to photo. Thread gingerbread kids on wire, curl wire ends and bend over arms. Screw eyes in heart cookies, thread raffia through eyes and tie ends in a bow. Hang cookies on arms. Spray with Clear sealer.

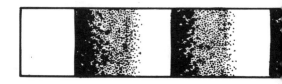

GINGERBREAD MAN GARLAND

While Visions of Sugar Plums danced in their heads..

BASE

Snowy, the Bird Man

BACK COVER PHOTO

MATERIALS:

2½" x 5" Black felt hat	Raffia
Small amount of greenery	5 small Brown feathers
Checkerboard stencil	Stencil brush
Pink powdered blush	Spanish moss
2½" x 24" of Teal check fabric	6 screw eyes
'Love Warms You…' rub-on saying	

WOOD PARTS:

Large snowman and base	6 birds
Acorn birdhouse	2 tall birdhouses
2 rounded birdhouses	Mosquito house
Three ¾" Black buttons	Sign
4" of ⅛" dowel	1½" of ¼" dowel

DECOART PAINT:

Buttermilk	Snow White	Ebony Black
Pumpkin	Desert Sand	French Grey Blue
Santa Red	Moon Yellow	Burnt Umber
Cranberry Wine	Sable Brown	Hauser Dark Green
Rookwood Red	Deep Midnight Blue	Weathered Wood

INSTRUCTIONS:

Trace pattern. Sharpen point of ¼" dowel for nose. Drill ¼" hole in face and one on each side of snowman for arms. Drill ⅛" holes in base and bottom of sign. Glue nose in face hole, let dry.

PAINT:

Snowman

Body - Buttermilk, shade French Grey Blue.

Eyes - Ebony Black, float Buttermilk in lower part. Add star highlight on right side with thinned Buttermilk.

Cheeks - rub on blush.

Nose - Pumpkin, shade base Rookwood Red.

Mouth - dot Ebony Black.

Heart - Cranberry Wine.

When dry, brush on Clear sealer and sprinkle with Glamour Dust.

Mosquito Birdhouse - Buttermilk, shade Sable Brown.

Roof - Rookwood Red.

Checks - Rookwood Red with #2 flat shader.

Birdhouse with star - Rookwood Red, shade Rookwood Red + Ebony Black.

Roof - Hauser Dark Green.

Star - Buttermilk.

Hole - Ebony Black, float Buttermilk.

Birdhouse with heart - Rookwood Red, shade Rookwood Red + Ebony Black.

Checks - Deep Midnight Blue with #6 flat shader.

Heart, roof, strokes - Desert Sand. Shade roof Rookwood Red + Ebony Black.

Tall Striped Birdhouse - Hauser Dark Green, shade Hauser Dark Green + Ebony Black.

Roof, stripes - Desert Sand, shade Sable Brown.

Hole - Ebony Black, float Buttermilk.

Tall Birdhouse - French Grey Blue, shade French Grey Blue + Ebony Black.

Roof, base - Rookwood Red. Shade roof Rookwood Red + Ebony Black.

Checks- Buttermilk with #2 flat shader

Stripe - Deep Midnight Blue.

Acorn Birdhouse - wash Burnt Umber, shade Ebony Black. Top - Moon Yellow, sponge Sable Brown.

Brown Birds - Sable Brown, shade Burnt Umber. Float wing Buttermilk.

Beak - Moon Yellow.

Eyes - dot Ebony Black, let dry. Dot Snow White.

Cardinals - Santa Red, shade around wing Ebony Black.

Front of face - Ebony Black.

Beak, eyes - Pumpkin.

Sign - Burnt Umber, let dry. Paint Weathered Wood, let dry. Paint Buttermilk.

Dowel - Burnt Umber.

Base - French Grey Blue, sponge Buttermilk, let dry. Stencil front Buttermilk.

ASSEMBLE:

Attach base to snowman. Make arms, glue in side holes. Glue ⅛" dowel in sign and base. Glue buttons on chest and hat on head. Glue Spanish moss, greenery and feathers on hat and base for nests. Glue birds referring to photo. Tie scarf around neck. Screw eyes into birdhouses, thread raffia though eyes and tie a bow. Hang birdhouses on arms. Spray with sealer

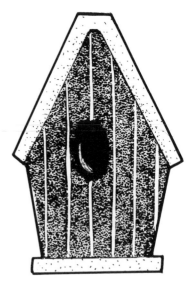

Sayings. Cut saying from a rub-on sheet, position on wood piece, rub with embossing tool to transfer Or draw saying with a marker pen..

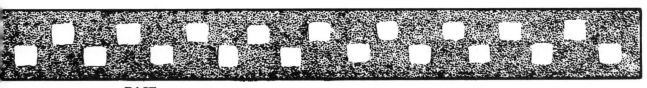

BASE

Mrs. Snow Teacher

BACK COVER PHOTO

MATERIALS:

Pink powdered blush
Small eraser
Small chalkboard
Heavy Black thread
½" x 6" strip of Red felt
'A+ Teacher' and 2 apple rub ons
Two 7" x 15" pieces of Red and a 2" square of Green fabric
Black and White fine-tip permanent pens

Grey curly crepe hair
Crystal Twinkles
2½" wire glasses
Green raffia

WOOD PARTS:

Large snowman and base
School bus
2 small rectangles
¾" button
Bird
1½" of ¼" dowel

Schoolhouse
Two 1" apples
Red crab apple
Red cherry apple
6" of ⅛" dowel

DECOART PAINT:

Buttermilk	Snow White	Ebony Black
Santa Red	Slate Grey	Leaf Green
Pumpkin	Rookwood Red	Uniform Blue
Cadmium Yellow	Burnt Umber	French Grey Blue

INSTRUCTIONS:

Trace patterns. Cut two 2" pieces for pencils and one 1" piece for chalk from ⅛" dowel. Sharpen point of ¼" dowel for nose and pencil points. Drill ¼" hole in face and one on each side of Santa for arms. Glue nose in face hole, let dry.

PAINT:

Teacher
  Body, base - Buttermilk, shade French Grey Blue.
  Eyes - Ebony Black, float Buttermilk in lower part. Add star highlight on right side with thinned Buttermilk.
  Cheeks - rub with blush.
  Nose - Pumpkin, shade base Rookwood Red.
  Mouth - dot Ebony Black.
Apples - Santa Red, shade Ebony Black + Santa Red.
  Highlight with thinned Snow White.
  Leaves - Leaf Green
  Stems - Burnt Umber.
Bus - Cadmium Yellow
  Windows, tires - Ebony Black, float Buttermilk.
  Hub cap - dot Cadmium Yellow.
  Sign - Slate Grey. Make letters and outline with Black pen.
Schoolhouse - Rookwood Red, shade Ebony Black.
  Door, windows - Ebony Black, outline Snow White.
  Roof - Slate Grey, line Ebony Black.
Slates
  Border - wash Burnt Umber.
  Slate - Ebony Black.
  Letters - White pen.
Pencils
  Centers - Cadmium Yellow.
  Erasers - Cadmium Yellow + Santa Red.
  Metal band - Slate Grey.
  Lead - Ebony Black.
Bird - French Grey Blue, shade wing Uniform Blue.
  Bead - Cadmium Yellow.
  Eye - dot Snow White, add tiny Ebony Black dot.
Chalk - Snow White.

Base - Ebony Black, make letters with White pen.
Large Slate
  Apples - rub on.
  Letters - Black and White pens and rub on.
Button - Snow White.
Spray with Clear sealer.

ASSEMBLE:

1. Coat: Cut coat pieces from Red fabric and heart from Green fabric using patterns. Using ½" seam allowance sew pieces together leaving a small opening, turn and sew opening shut. Cut small slit for arms. Sew heart on coat. Place coat on Teacher, sew button through both thicknesses.

2. Attach base to Teacher. Make arms, glue in side holes. Glue eraser, cherry and crab apples, large slate, one pencil, bird and chalk referring to photo. Glue hair on head, felt strip around head and one pencil in hair. Tie thread on glasses, hang around neck. Screw eyes in remaining small wood pieces, thread raffia through eyes, tie bows and hang on arms.

FOLD DOWN FOR COLLAR

FOLD

Mrs.
Snow

Teaching is
Touching a Life
forever.

A+ Teacher

COAT
CUT 1 FROM
RED FABRIC

STITCH LINE

School

Wood Parts Directory

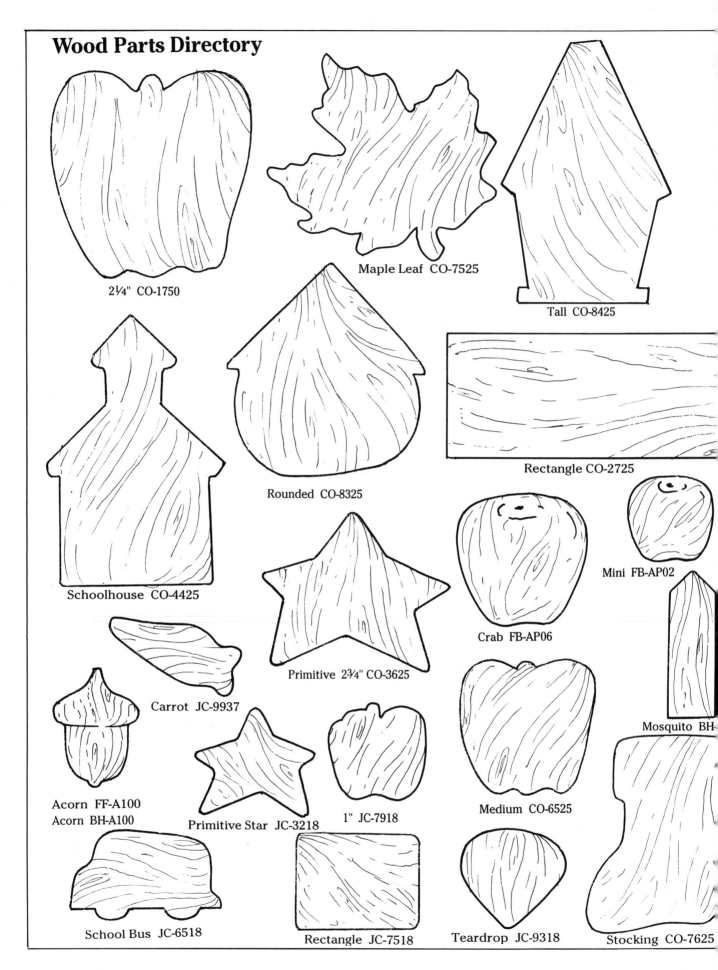

2¼" CO-1750

Maple Leaf CO-7525

Tall CO-8425

Rounded CO-8325

Rectangle CO-2725

Schoolhouse CO-4425

Primitive 2¾" CO-3625

Crab FB-AP06

Mini FB-AP02

Carrot JC-9937

Acorn FF-A100
Acorn BH-A100

Primitive Star JC-3218

1" JC-7918

Medium CO-6525

Mosquito BH-

School Bus JC-6518

Rectangle JC-7518

Teardrop JC-9318

Stocking CO-7625